HOW TO LIVE & DIE WITH CALIFORNIA PROBATE

A LAYMAN'S GUIDE TO UNDERSTANDING PROBATE IN CALIFORNIA

John B. Palley, Esq.

{Certified Specialist in Estate Planning, Trust and Probate Law as Determined by the State Bar of California Board of Legal Specialization.}

ISBN: 978-1-941645-57-4

Designed and Published by:

Speakeasy Publications
73-03 Bell Blvd #10
Oakland Gardens, N.Y. 11364
www.SpeakeasyMarketingInc.com
888-225-8594

DISCLAIMER

NOTE TO READER: Please remember that the forms and information in here are accurate as of the date of publishing. The state Judicial Council forms change, laws change, Courts change, etc... so please bear all this in mind. What you read here is a good guide for you but you should double check the Judicial Council forms on-line, the probate code and the written and unwritten rules at the specific probate court. Also, please remember that I am not your attorney nor am I giving you legal advice. I am merely providing an overview of the probate process.

John B. Palley, Attorney at Law
Meissner Joseph & Palley, Inc.

1555 River Park Drive #108
Sacramento, CA 95815
916-920-5983
www.californiaprobate.info

2240 Douglas Blvd., Suite 150
Roseville, California 95661
916-774-0560
www.californiaprobate.info

CLIENT TESTIMONIALS

"*Mr. Palley was so helpful, kind, courteous and very interested in my issues. Mr. Palley took the time to investigate my issues and respond to me before making any conclusions. He made sure he knew what he was talking about and not just a "for instance" kind of lawyer as the one I had spoken to before Mr. Palley. I am so glad I found Mr. Palley and would highly recommend him for anyone that wants an awesome lawyer that is truly interested in protecting their best interests.*"   **- Amelia**

....

"*John Palley provides "Top Shelf" service!!! He assisted my family with a Living trust and Will. The process was easy and turn key. John took the time to understand our situation and put together a program that put our family in the best position to be protected. His knowledge and responsiveness is second to none. I highly recommend working with John. He is a man of integrity and professionalism.*"   **- Gary**

....

"*It was a pleasure working alongside Mr. Palley on a complex and hostile probate matter. Since then I have referred clients to Mr. Palley and remain comfortable doing so based upon his knowledge, experience and people skills.*"   **- Scott**

....

"*We had a surprise on who was and was not on the title to the house after my step-father died. John gave us clear, actionable advice within an hour after I sent an email to him. I felt like I knew what legal grounds we stood on and direction about what to do next. Thank you John!*"   **- Teddy**

....

"*My family had hired an attorney that had completely misinformed us about the position we were in and what we were entitled to regarding our probate/estate case. Wanting a second opinion, I emailed John and he was quick to respond and dead on accurate with his information to me. He definitely knows this area of law. If he was closer to Orange County I would've fired our attorney and hired him.*"   **- Traci**

PRO·BATE

/'prō,bāt/

noun

1. the official proving of a will.

"The will was in probate"

TERMINOLOGY

➢ **Administrator** - Person named to administer the probate if not named in will

➢ **Court Reporter** - The person who types notes of what is said in Court and does not exist in all probate court rooms

➢ **Decedent** - The person who died

➢ **Executor** - Person named to administer the probate in the will

➢ **File Examiner** - Is typically an attorney, but sometimes a non-attorney, who works at the court and advises the Judge on each case

➢ **Judge** - The probate Judge is a Superior Court Judge who is in charge of the process

➢ **Lawyer** - Typically the Personal Representative is represented by their own legal counsel

➢ **Personal Representative** - Includes Executor, Administrator and Special Administrator

➢ **Probate Referee** – State appointed official who appraises probate assets

➢ **Special Administrator** - Person named to act on behalf of the estate on an emergency or temporary basis

TABLE OF CONTENTS

AUTHOR INTRODUCTION

John Palley handles probate cases throughout California and has been an attorney since 1994 focusing on trust and estates throughout his years in practice. John is a "Super Lawyer" as determined by Superlawyers.com, he has been rated "AV" by Martindale Hubbell (lawyers.com),  he has been rated as "Lead Counsel Rated" (lawinfo.com) and he has a 10.0 rating on AVVO.com. Additionally, he is a Certified Specialist in Estate Planning, Trust and Probate Law as determined by the State Bar of California Board of Legal Specialization and has held that credential since 2008.

John is a past Sacramento Bee estate planning expert and has been quoted in other publications including Forbes.com, Private Wealth Magazine and Grandparents.com. John is a partner at Meissner, Joseph & Palley, Inc. which is an AV rated firm serving California since 1979.

Intro To Readers

My job is to explain the court side of the process in detail to help you better navigate the system. There are other books on probate but it's my feeling they talk too much about the forms and not enough about the actual process.

As a person who has taught classes on probate and estate planning law at UC Davis Extension, NBI and McQuillan, I think I am well versed to write a book to help educate you on the whole process. Please be my student, but don't worry, there is no test at the end!

EXPERIENCE OF MEISSNER, JOSEPH & PALLEY LAW FIRM IN PROBATE

Attorney John B. Palley has been an estate planning and probate attorney since 1994. He has been with the Meissner, Joseph & Palley law firm since 1999. He focuses 100% on probate and estate planning matters.

The firm itself has been around since 1979 and focuses heavily on probate and estate planning. Attorney Palley is a Certified Specialist in Estate Planning, Trust and Probate law as determined by the State Bar of California Board of Legal Specialization. In addition to  passing a second bar exam, Attorney Palley also passed the background exam that's given to attorneys and judges to make sure that they are certified specialists. He has also taught classes in estate planning and probate and has been handling these matters throughout the state of California since 1994.

Probate Cases Handled By John B. Palley In His Career

Attorney John B. Palley has handled a significant number of probate cases throughout his career. Beyond the quantity, it's also the fact that he gets these cases done in a timely fashion and that's really the key. As a result of having resolved so many cases, Attorney Palley has been in court countless times where he sat through other probate cases.

He has seen what other attorneys do, good and bad, and has certainly learned a lot from that as well.

Counties Served By Meissner, Joseph & Palley

The main office of Meissner, Joseph & Palley is in Sacramento with branch offices in Yolo County and Placer County. The local counties in the Sacramento region are certainly their strengths and at the time of writing this book have active probates in at least ten different counties and can handle probate matters in every county in California.

In the State of California, attorneys can appear in court telephonically through a service called Court Call. Court Call works excellently for probate matters which tend to be non-adversarial. Probate cases are more administrative in nature and it is helpful to be available to answer the judges' questions and that can easily be done through the court call telephonic appearance. This makes it easy for an experienced probate attorney to handle probate matters throughout the state.

Unique Attributes Of Meissner, Joseph & Palley In Handling Probate Matters

Without a doubt, experience is what sets the firm of Meissner, Joseph & Palley, and in particular John Palley, apart from all other law  firms. Mr. Palley has personally handled nearly a thousand probate cases, if not more. Not many law firms can match that know-how! In addition to Mr. Palley and the other experienced attorneys of the firm, in recent years one of the associate attorneys of Meissner, Joseph & Palley is an attorney who formerly worked for a local probate court as a staff attorney where they advised the probate Judge on matters before the court. That attorney was with the Court for over 25 years! The second major factor is efficiency. The office of Meissner, Joseph & Palley have systems in place to get things done quickly! Most people want their probate completed in seven months and we aim to achieve that. They want to receive their share of the estate, to move past the death of a loved one, and get on with the next stages of life.

The experience and efficiency of Meissner, Joseph & Palley helps accomplish that in the majority of cases.

Types Of Probate

Probate is based on old English common law and is generally defined as the clearing of title to assets. The word itself stems from the 1460's.

Basically, the decedent's will or his last wishes or instructions should be carried out upon death. To probate that will is to carry out their instructions or their wishes. That is done in the probate  court, which is the place that manages the process. Probate protects the decedent's wishes and makes sure that they are followed.

There is a probate judge who oversees everything, monitors the proceedings and helps to ensure that those wishes are followed. Generally, the wishes are demonstrated by a written will, which is called the last will and testament. If they don't have a will, it's what some people call a presumed will or, technically, "intestate succession."

If a person dies without a will, the state has come up with the rules of intestate succession. These rules are the state's version of a will for people who die without one. An attorney will run it through the probate court to help make sure that those mandates of the state are carried out.

Probate is a broad term. The probate court handles a number of different types of cases, all generally relating to two main issues; one is people dying, which is the majority of cases and the other is people who have become incapacitated or are unable to protect themselves, such as guardianships for young people.

Alternatives To A Full Probate

Generally speaking, a full probate is required in many cases. However, before a full probate is filed, all of the alternate options that are available should be explored, to make it as efficient as possible, both with time and money. An attorney should not waste the client's money as they have an ethical duty to the client. A full probate is definitely the main option that may be required but it's helpful to look at the other options available to see if a more economically efficient option would work.

The main threshold, in California, is if the assets in question are $150,000 or less, then a full probate can be avoided. In that situation there are some limited procedures that can be utilized to clear title to assets and pass them to the rightful people. Though not a full probate you are still in probate court. In some cases, with trusts, you may still need to go to probate court after death. However, often it's not a full probate and it is cheaper and more efficient if the facts support it. This is what is called a "Heggstad Petition" or what some may now call an "Ukkestad petition" after another case came down in this area of law.

A Heggstad Petition is a way of transferring assets into a trust if this were not done properly before death. The office of Meissner, Joseph & Palley handles a large number of these cases as well. In total, the goal is to transfer assets to the rightful  people after death. More information is available on their website at www.HeggstadPetition.com.

Tentative Cost Of A Full Probate In California

The general rule in California is that a full probate is required when assets exceed $150,000. However, cases where the assets are $150,000 or less can still require trips to the probate court. Though an attorney is not required it is a very good idea to hire one to assist with matters in the probate court with the probate judge.

Any real property owned in California requires a certain level of probate court work unless something has been done before death to avoid it such as a living trust. In fact, one abbreviated probate court procedure is for real property that is worth $50,000 or less. This procedure uses affidavits that are filed with the probate court clerk and generally do not go in front of the Judge. Although there are not a lot of these done in California, those would be timeshares and pieces of real estate where small fractions have been divided up.

COMMON ISSUES FACED BY PRACTITIONERS IN PROBATE PROCESS

There is definitely a broad range of assistance provided to clients going through the probate process. The main objective when representing a fiduciary, the person representing the personal representative, is to help make the probate process as easy as possible. The attorney's job  is to protect and provide service to aid in moving through the procedure in the minimum amount of time. All the while, the attorney is there to advise the personal representative of pitfalls to be careful of.

It's not as simple as filling out a number of forms. It is more complex and may even involve negotiating with banks, creditors and others. There can be local tax issues, dealing with other attorneys that might represent beneficiaries, and clearly explaining everything to the court. All this is done so that the probate process can continue toward a proper conclusion.

Common Misconceptions About The Probate Process

The most common misconception people have regarding probate is that it takes years. It certainly can take that long, however, if you hire an attorney who knows the system and is efficient, it should not. Seven months is the target timeline for the attorneys at Meissner, Joseph & Palley. Seven months is the minimum and that is our goal in each and every probate case unless there is a reason to spend more time or something happens beyond our control.

The other thing commonly misunderstood is thinking that probate is a tax. It is not officially a "tax," though there is a cost that is based on a percentage of the assets. Most of those assets, or that percentage,  does not go to the government; instead it's actually for attorney fees. It may seem worse than a tax to some people, but it's not a tax in the official sense.

Another mistaken belief is that a lot of people think probate is totally unnecessary and that it's a wasted process. In some cases that might actually be true. For example, there are families that are friendly, they do the right thing and it truly is a shame that they have to go through the time consuming probate process. However, there are other situations where having the attorneys and judge involved help to keep people honest. The probate process is necessary and is useful in those cases.

Reasons Why People Have Trouble With Probate Process

The office of Meissner, Joseph & Palley has been handling probate cases for more than 20 years. They have had countless clients who have had trouble with these matters before hiring Meissner, Joseph & Palley. The most common scenarios having unfavorable results include people who hire an inexperienced attorney who is only just learning the probate process. Though it  might not always be difficult, there is certainly an art to probate and when you have handled hundreds of cases, you learn the pitfalls to avoid. Inexperienced attorneys, paralegal services, and attorneys who practice many areas of law do not necessarily know those particulars.

Unfortunately, in probate when you make a mistake, it usually results in a continuance that could be anywhere from 4 weeks to even 12 weeks. If the continuances start to pile up, it's going to take a lot more time. Inexperienced attorneys are certainly more susceptible to such problems.

Likewise, some people try to do the probate themselves and this can create huge nightmares and literally can take years. People may file the wrong documents or, once they do figure out the right document, fill it out improperly. Mistakes create continuances and that time starts to pile up.

Lastly, the worst horror stories involve the unscrupulous people who seem to come out of the woodwork. This could include family, friends and even strangers. Keep in mind probate is a public record and unfortunately people take advantage of that. People looking to make a fast buck might contact those named in a probate and try to benefit off of a person in any way that they can. There are countless things that could happen and they all contribute to the awful stories that you hear about probate.

Having an experienced probate attorney can definitely help to reduce these problems.

IS PROBATE NECESSARY?

Probate is necessary for orderly, as well as, structured management and division of assets and liabilities. It is also essential to ensure assets go to the right people. Without the structure of probate, without the probate code which governs probate, and without the judge to make sure the laws are applied properly and the right process is followed, it's certainly possible that the wrong people could receive the money.

At the end, that's really what matters; you want the assets and money of the person who died to go to the rightful creditors, individuals, agencies and charities and probate helps to regulate that process.

Does All Of A Deceased Person's Property Go Through The Probate Process?

For a person who has not done proper estate planning, a majority or all assets go through probate. Again, if proper planning has not been done, technically this does include all of the assets, down to the smallest items of personal property. For example, the office of Meissner, Joseph & Palley had one case a couple of years back where they had inventoried every single item someone had. They literally had items on their inventory that the probate referee valued at 50 cents but they made sure to include every single asset in that probate to avoid any problems. While it is not common to appraise everything down to that level, in some cases it is necessary and advisable.

Can Having A Living Trust Help Avoid Probate?

A living trust is definitely the best way to avoid the probate process. When the living trust is set up properly, all the assets are put into the trust, or tied to the trust in some fashion. The  administration of a trust can literally be weeks instead of months and the attorney's fees can be hundreds instead of thousands. This is definitely the way to go when possible.

There are other options for avoiding probate that may be appropriate in limited circumstances. Those include the new revocable transfer on death deed which started in California on January 1st, 2016. Utilizing joint tenancies is another option to avoid probate in some situations where real estate is involved. For non-real estate assets payable on death accounts can also be used. Generally, the best way to avoid probate in California though, is through a living trust.

What Are Some Common Hurdles That Someone Might Face During The Probate Process?

There are a number of issues that come up in probate. In fact, a probate is like a hurdles race. There are different hurdles that need to be jumped over throughout this race and most of those hurdles are court dates. There are certain events that need to happen at a certain time.

These hurdles can be made larger if the procedures are not being done properly because that's when another continuance happens. A continuance is going to delay the probate process and that should be avoided wherever and whenever possible. Another  issue is the government cutbacks in the last few years have created severe understaffing at most of the courts in California. That has made it significantly more difficult to file papers, to look in the court files, to get court dates in a timely manner, etc. The understaffing has created a whole host of additional hurdles in the probate process.

Lastly, the reality is that there are official forms that are to be used for much of the probate process. However, there are also unofficial forms, or unofficial rules. Those are not written anywhere and are just procedures that happen during the probate process. If you do not know what to expect, and you do not look ahead for that hurdle, that can be a problem and a significant barrier to getting the process done properly and in a timely manner. An experienced probate attorney can see the whole hurdle race and plan ahead for the hurdles before they arrive.

THE PEOPLE INVOLVED IN THE
PROBATE PROCESS

The most common scenario is that the attorney represents the personal representative. A personal representative is a broad term that includes the executor or the administrator. It's basically the fiduciary or  the person handling the administration of the estate. This includes individuals, family members, friends, as well as other people who the decedent knew.

It might be professional fiduciaries in some cases, such as banks, other lawyers or accountants. In fact, California has licensed professional fiduciaries which is a good option to consider. More information can be found on licensed professional fiduciaries at www.PFAC-PRO.org.

The attorney will essentially represent anyone who is handling the administration of the estate. In a few cases, the attorney will take a beneficiary representation to help guide a beneficiary through the probate process to make sure they are being treated fairly by the personal representative.

Main Players In A Probate Case

In a probate, there are many players. Certainly, the probate judge is the master of the whole situation. He or she is the person in control and will be overseeing the decedent's case going through the court system.

The decedent is the person who has died. There is also going to be an executor or administrator who is the person who will administer the estate. That person will generally have an attorney who is often called the probate attorney. Most courts in California have a file examiner. That is usually an attorney who works at the courthouse, who reviews the file and advises the judge on what to do. Lastly, there is the beneficiary, who is the person who will ultimately receive the assets. Those are the main players in a probate.

Difference Between An Executor, Administrator And A Personal Representative

A personal representative is the term generally used in the California probate code. An executor is a person who is named in the decedent's will to administer the affairs.

An administrator is very similar with an executor. However, the term is used for either a decedent who does not have a will or if the people named in the will as the executor cannot serve or shouldn't serve. In those situations an administrator is named.

The other option that is used in some cases is called a special administrator. A special administrator is going to be used on a limited basis in emergency situations to keep things moving before the full executor or administrator can be appointed. An example of a situation where a special administrator might be used is if the decedent's house is in foreclosure and facing a foreclosure sale very soon.

Difference Between An Heir And A Beneficiary

The heir and the beneficiary are the people that ultimately receive the money and assets in a case. An heir is typically a blood relative of the decedent, or is the next of kin. If a person dies without a will, California probate code section 6400 will then determine who the next of kin is. That is, who the heirs-at-law are. If a person has a will, they are  going to name recipients to receive their assets. The person named in a will is the beneficiary. In total, both the heir and the beneficiary are the ones who the probate will ultimately benefit by giving them the money and assets at the conclusion of the probate process.

TIMELINE FOR THE PROBATE PROCESS

During the probate process, the attorney is going to help lead the personal representative from the beginning to the end. The process starts with filling out some forms and filing them in the court. The next step will be appearing at the appropriate court dates to talk to the judge and answer any questions they have. The attorney will continue to calendar the events throughout the process to lead you to the end of that hurdles race.

The big items that are done in a probate are gathering of all the assets, determining all liabilities, taxes, and who the heirs are, as well as determining who should receive the money and then giving the money to that person at the end. That is the probate process.

The Standard Timeline For A Probate Case

In late 1996, I put up my first website dedicated to providing legal information on the internet. At that point, I had a timeline that I called the six months' probate timeline. The situation over the years, particularly in the last ten years with budget cuts, has now changed that timeline to seven months which is the minimum that a probate is going to take.

Following the timeline, if you file a probate on day one, approximately six weeks later, you will have your first court date. Assuming you are successful, you will then start the four-month probate period. At the end of the four months, you can file your final petition if everything is done. Hopefully, the final hearing is held approximately six weeks later and approved. In total, it's about seven months or longer. It's not going to be shorter than that in California at this time.

California Probate Process Time-Line

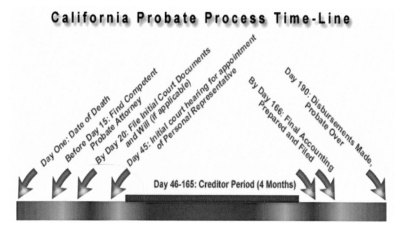

Probate should take approximately seven months. Unfortunately, a lot of attorneys do not aim for that same time frame. They do not have the same focus on getting it done and it literally does take well over a year, if not years, to get the process completed. The office of Meissner, Joseph & Palley pride themselves on completing most of their probate cases in very close to just seven months.

Reasons Why Probate Takes Longer Than The Seven-Month Mark

There are many reasons for delays in probate. The most common is when people don't use the right forms. They use out of date forms or they use the wrong forms. Many forms seem very similar but are completely different.

Although the process of filling the forms is pretty straightforward, if it's your first or second or even fifth time doing it, you really have to think  through these questions. When people fail to mark the forms correctly or complete the forms completely, they then will end up with delays.

Another factor to the timeline is the sooner you start the process, the sooner you finish. Again, you're aiming for seven months but it's seven months from when you start it. If you hire an experienced attorney like John Palley before 10 a.m. or 11 a.m. on any weekday, he should have it filed in probate court on the next business day and in some cases, even the same day.

You need to have efficiency like that if you are aiming for your seven months. If you don't have an attorney with that mentality, it's going to take longer.

Other issues that can delay the probate process are missing local forms or local rules.
Each court has different requirements and you need to read the local rules to make sure that you get each thing

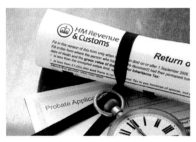

done properly for that court. Even though there are a lot of state standardized systems and forms in place, there are others that are local. You need to get all of those done to make sure that you don't cause unnecessary delays.

California probate code 8200 says that if you have possession of somebody's will and have knowledge of their death, you have 30 days from the receipt of the knowledge of death to lodge the will in court. Failure to do  so can actually lead to penalties for the person holding the will. However, there isn't really an official deadline for finishing the probate.

Some courts track a time and aim for probates to be done within about a year. However, the majority of courts in California do not and do not have deadlines. If a person is not paying attention, it literally can take years to finish, which could be quite stressful. Likewise, if you are in a county that does track cases it can be stressful to make sure you meet their deadlines.

What's The Use Of A Surety Bond?

A surety bond is aimed at protecting the beneficiaries or heirs of an estate as well as creditors and even the government from a personal representative who absconds with the money. Although this is not very common, if the executor or the administrator decides that they really should have all that money, maybe they run off to a foreign country with all the money or they gamble it away. A surety bond is similar to insurance to replenish the money into the estate after an administrator steals the money.

Unfortunately, surety bonds do not work quite as well as insurance. The surety bond companies tend to fight the payment when they are ordered to pay. In this author's experience they do not just write a check and thus it is really not great insurance. Instead the bond company may fight payment for months, or even years, and only pay if the court orders it. There are other protections that may be better or in addition to a surety bond.

Steps Required To Get Protections In Place At The Beginning Of A Probate

If you're a beneficiary and someone else has applied or filed to become the personal representative of the estate, protections will be needed. If you've seen the petition filed and if you don't fully trust that person implicitly, then you need to think about putting some protections in place for yourself.

The first thing is if you are asked to sign a bond waiver, which goes back to the surety bond discussion above, you probably shouldn't sign. That's because although the surety bond is not great insurance, it is some insurance. There are two ways it provides some protection:

First, the personal representative has to have good credit and own real estate, or have a cosigner with those things, before the surety bond company will issue the bond. That puts some protection in place.

Second, even if it's not great insurance, that bond does provide some insurance even if you might have to fight to get it paid.

If there is a will, then you won't be asked to waive the bond but you could file something in court that expresses your concerns. Perhaps you think that a bond is appropriate even though the will waives it and possibly the judge will listen to that. Other things  you can do, might be to ask the court that all money has to be put into what are called court ordered blocked accounts. Or even ask the Judge to specify that the Personal

---

Representative cannot take possession of assets without a specific court order.

Court ordered blocked accounts basically means that the personal representative cannot touch the money without a specific court order. It's going to make it significantly harder for them to gamble the money away or anything like that. Other things you could do, would be to advise the judge of your concerns and hopefully they will not give the administrator or the executor full authority under the Independent Administration of Estates Act or IAEA. Instead, maybe they will give them limited authority, which makes it a little harder for them to take action without court involvement or at least limit the selling of real property to require Court involvement.

The judge could even give the administrator or the executor no authority at all under the Independent Administration of Estates Act, just general authority. However, you will need to take action with the court to have any of those restrictions put in place.  Another protection is you always want to file a request for special notice and make sure to serve a copy on all of the parties in the case and their attorneys. You will check the box that says you want to receive all filed documents. When that is done, the attorney is supposed to send you a copy of anything filed in Court. That will help keep you informed on what's going on and keeping informed definitely helps protect you to know what's happening.

TECHNICAL TERMS USED IN THE PROBATE PROCESS

In a California probate case, the most common scenario is that the personal representative will have either full or limited IAEA powers. When an attorney is representing the fiduciary, they want them to have full authority because that full authority makes it as

easy as possible for them to take all actions on behalf of the decedent with as little court involvement as possible. That allows the case to move along a little quicker and a little smoother.

In some cases, the attorney might only ask for limited authority. This can be the case if they are representing a beneficiary and they want that personal representative to report back to court. For example, having limited authority means that they can't sell real estate without directly going back to court and getting the court involved. There are pros and cons to that but at least you know that the judge is involved with the process and it helps provide some confidence that the personal representative is doing things properly.

Initial Documents That An Attorney Prepares For A New Client

An efficient probate attorney will try to have the first round of documents ready to file the same day, hopefully within a few hours of the first meeting with the client. First, there is always going to be a written fee agreement that is the agreement between the attorney and the client as to what the attorney fees are going to be.

The attorney will then prepare a petition for probate, the duties and liabilities, the confidential supplement to duties and liabilities and they will prepare "letters," which is the name of a document. Lastly, they will prepare bond waivers if they are required. Those are the documents that an attorney will typically prepare initially to get the process started.

What's The Use Of A Probate Petition?

A probate petition is laying out all the facts for the court. These facts will include information such as who died, when they died, where they died and who the family is. If there is a will, the attorney would include a copy of the will attached to the petition. The petition will include a list of all people who are entitled to notice.

The probate petition is basically laying everything out so that the probate court knows what is going on. It will also include the asset values or estimated values of the assets, not the specific assets. The

PROBATE

questions can be tricky in the petition. A good attorney always goes over all the questions with their client to make sure that they understand what they are signing under the penalty of perjury to be the truth. Sometimes they might have to do family tree research or things like that before the probate is filed but that's a rare instance.

"Letters" is the document that allows the personal representative to stand in the decedent's shoes and take action on their behalf. Whatever action is needed, "letters" is the document that will allow it to happen. Most commonly, people call it letters testamentary.

Letters testamentary means that there is a will and the letters are essentially supporting that will; it's what the executor would use to prove their authority. Letters of administration are going to be used when there is no will and an administrator is involved. The powers are going to be the same either way but it's just a slightly different name for the document.

The Tentative Calendar Note System
Used By Most Courts In California

One of the nice features in California probates are that the court file examiner will review the file before the court date in most cases and advise the judge of any issues. Even before that, they typically post the concerns online in many counties. There might be a deficiency, such as maybe you forgot to check a box or maybe the court just has a question about something. They will post those questions so that the attorney can review them and then file an appropriate response to get it fixed before the court date.

Some courts file those as early as three or four weeks before the court date, which gives you plenty of time to fix the problem. Unfortunately, others put up their tentative ruling at two, three or even four o'clock in the afternoon the day before the court date, which in most cases makes it hard to fix if there is a problem. However, it at least lets you know what to expect going in.

Fixing Or Replying To Deficiencies And Tentative Rulings Or Calendar Notes

Going back to your goal of a seven-month probate, each court date is precious. You want to do everything you possibly can to get your case approved. You want to avoid having your case continued. Hopefully, when you read the calendar notes or the tentative ruling, it says RFA, which means "Recommended For Approval." In some counties it might say "pre-grant" or "pre-approved," and that's certainly your goal.

Unfortunately, there are cases which involve complex questions which need to be resolved. You have to figure out how you can respond to the questions and what is the best way of getting it approved. The worst way is to show up in court and orally tell the judge what the answer is to fix a deficiency. Most courts do not want to just hear about it live in court. They want something in writing so there is a written court record of exactly what has been done.

It's also a matter of figuring out which of the different procedures is best for fixing the deficiency. A common approach is called a "Response to Calendar Notes." The lawyer drafts the document and it is literally titled "response to calendar notes." They would indicate what the calendar note is and they will note the reply that hopefully fixes or answers the question.

The person or client who wants to be the personal representative, under the penalty of perjury, will sign that the "fixes" in the document are correct.

Occasionally, the question is minor and more of an administrative thing. In those cases, the attorney can actually sign it. However, again, to ensure approval at the court date, having the client sign or the proposed personal representative sign under penalty of perjury is the best.

If there are more significant problems, then in some cases, they might call it a supplement to a petition or even an amended petition.

A supplement to a petition is going to have more of a legally significant response. It would probably have actual legal answers and the client should sign that under the penalty of perjury. The other option is an "amended petition." This is typically only done by the attorney when he or she has taken over for another attorney or an individual as a *pro per*. Filing pro per means they have filed on their own without an attorney.

However, when there are too many problems, then a supplement won't work. Instead a new petition, called an "Amended Petition," is needed. There are two reasons to avoid the Amended Petition. First, most courts will require another $435 filing fee. Secondly, they will usually give a new court date, which is going to be another six or eight weeks out.

Since court dates are precious, you want to do everything you can to save the court date, and get the problem fixed. You want to treat those calendar notes very carefully and do everything you can to remedy the situation.

BASIC FACTS ABOUT THE PROBATE PROCESS

The first thing to understand is knowing who the attorney represents. If there are three kids involved, but only one of them is going to be the personal representative, then they should ask the attorney: "Who do you represent? Do I need my own attorney?"

The attorney then needs to ask the client, "Do you want to be the personal representative or are you okay with a brother or sister or someone else doing it?" You want to ask yourself if you really trust that person to handle it. Those are the things to look at. Who is the attorney representing? Do you want to be that personal representative yourself even though it's a pretty big headache? Do you really trust your sibling or another person to be the administrator?

The Four-Month Probate Period

The four months' probate period starts the day letters of administration or letters testamentary are issued. Either way, it is the day the personal representative takes over and now stands in the decedent's shoes to take action. That's really the heart of a probate. It is four months, at a minimum, before the final petition can be filed. As the attorneys goal is seven months in total it is important to keep the probate period to exactly, or close to, the four months.

The administrator or the personal representative is going to immediately begin trying to marshal all assets. They will collect all assets and will look through the decedent's paperwork, tax returns, checkbook and anything else they can, to try to find out what assets are out there. Likewise, the personal representative needs to figure out what creditors and  liabilities there are. They will go through bank statements, records, and anything possible to figure out that information. That is going to be key. In summation, the big issues are: assets, creditors, taxes and who to distribute the assets to.

Usually, it is recommended that the personal representative hire a certified public accountant (or CPA) who has experience doing this type of tax work. In some cases, an enrolled agent (or EA) is also perfectly acceptable. However, the key is to hire a tax professional and not to do it yourself.

The other important thing is determining the heirs. In most cases, it's very straightforward. Mom died, she has two kids so everyone knows who the heirs are. In other cases, it might be more difficult to ascertain for a variety of reasons.

For example, if a person dies who had no close relatives, no children, no siblings, no nieces, no nephews, yet the family tree turns out to be quite large. The attorney will file a petition to ascertain which of those people are the rightful heirs and in what percentages.

To decide how the estate should be divided up, the attorney will actually file a petition for heirship to have the court tell them that it agrees with what their conclusions were. Assuming the Judge agrees the Court will issue a Court order advising the Personal Representative who to distribute the money to at the conclusion of probate.

If all goes according to plan, at the end of the four months, the attorney is ready to file the final petition and show how the money should be distributed. Unfortunately, these difficult cases that involve heirship generally are going to take a little longer. However, the goal is still four months for the probate period and seven months in total.

Outcome Expected Upon Completion Of
The Probate Process

Assuming things are on track there should be a check or other division of assets that benefits each of the recipients, the heirs or the beneficiaries. Ultimately, that's what it's about. If money never does come, then there has probably been some sort of a problem.

Ultimately, it's getting the money distributed, to the right people, so that the family can close the door on the painful memories. That's what you are trying to accomplish. If all goes right this should be approximately seven months after you initiate the probate process.

LETTERS IN PROBATE AND FILING CLAIMS

When a personal representative has the letters, they essentially stand in the decedent's shoes; that means they literally can do anything that the decedent could have done while they were alive. That could mean going to the bank and accessing bank accounts and getting that money into an estate account. It might mean going to the bank and looking for a safe deposit box. It might mean selling the decedent's house or timeshare or other real estate. It means they can do anything!

It might also include dealing with liabilities, negotiating with creditors, and satisfying claims like credit card bills. In general, this is the time to review everything to ensure it is accurate. A lot of times, there is a fraud later in life or even after death, where people have used a credit card. This should get vetted during the probate process.

The personal representative will then need to make sure that the bill is correct before it gets paid or in some cases it might involve negotiating a reduction of those creditor claims. It's basically anything that the decedent could have done while they were alive. The person who has letters is in charge!

Filing Creditor Claims In Probate

A creditor, a person who is owed money by the decedent, has a couple of different options to enforce their claim. The primary claims are broken down into three main categories.

The first is going to be any money that a creditor thinks they are owed from something that happened before the person died. People get forgetful in paying their bills. It could be the gardener who files a claim for six months of  gardening services or anything like that. It could be people that are owed money, for other services rendered before death, such as a caretaker.

The second big thing is funeral expenses. The costs of cremation or burial service, or paying a religious leader, whatever it might be; all of those things would be done on a separate creditor claim form.

Thirdly, there are the costs of administration. That is going to be other expenses that come up after death. These expenses are probably going to be paying the mortgage, paying the utility bills, and things like that.

There are three broad categories. For the first two, i.e. claims from before death and funeral expenses, a creditor's claim form is used and there is a judicial council form to be used. The third, the costs of administration, is more of an attorney drafted form that should be used. However, the key  is filing those claims, especially the creditor's claim form for pre-death and for funeral, within four months of letters issuing.

As stated above, it is crucial that the creditor's claim forms for pre-death expenses and funeral expenses get filed within four months of letters issuing. If the process of filing is delayed, a person could lose the right to collect the money they are owed in some cases. If you think you are owed money you should file a claim in Court. Do not delay!

There are two main tax returns. The first is going to be the final 1040, that's going to be due April 15th the year after death. This means that if a person dies on July 1st, 2015, the final 1040 will then be due April 15th of 2016.

The other one is going to be the 1041 fiduciary return. The fiduciary return runs on a fiscal year so that's going to start from the date of death forward for 12 months. If July 1st is used as a date of death, it's going to start on that day and go for a year.

Typically, one 1040 and one 1041 are filed in most probate cases that have ended in a timely fashion. However, there are other situations that can arise. Most typically when there is fighting involved, the probate case may take a few years. In that case, there would be multiple 1041s, one for each fiscal year.

Lastly, the other tax return that is sometimes required is a 706, which is the estate tax return. That's typically required in larger estates. Currently, the tax law allows for approximately five and a half million dollars to be passed tax free without the filing of that 706 return. However, there are some large probate cases where the 706 would be needed and that's supposed to be filed within nine months of death.

Another common tax that is seen in probate cases is property taxes. That is, California real estate taxes relating to a change of ownership. This is an annual tax. There is a form to file with the county assessor as soon as possible called an Estate Change in Ownership. This is especially important when it is a transfer where the decedent is transferring property to their child. In a parent to child transfer it is very important that the proper forms get filed with the county assessor right away. This would be a BOE-58 which is available on the county assessor websites as well as the California BOE website.

W-9 Form In The Probate Process

A W-9 is an IRS form that each heir or each beneficiary is asked to fill out. It shows what their social security number is, which is needed to provide to the estate accountant. When they file the 1041 fiduciary return, the income tax, which is typically not huge in a probate case, gets apportioned amongst the beneficiaries.

You can give approximately five and a half million dollars tax free during life or at death or in combination. However, there could still be an income tax. For example, if during the course of a probate administration, there is $1,000 of income and there are two beneficiaries; each would be attributed $500 of that income for their own personal 1040. That W9 form is needed to make sure that the correct social security number gets taxed for that income.

The Tax ID Number In the Probate Process

The tax ID number (TIN), also called an employer identification number (EIN), takes over for the decedent's social security number. Any business entity, like a corporation or certain trusts or probate estates in this case, have their own tax identification number. This is for all financial action and all transactions that happened during the course of administration. The tax ID number will be used for reporting purposes.

A probate bank account will be opened in the estate. The tax ID number of the estate will be used rather than anybody's personal social security number. If the house is sold, there are certain tax forms that are filed; those are going to use this tax ID number.

It's basically just a way to keep the IRS and the California Franchise Tax Board informed of the taxable transactions that happen during the estate administration. In most cases it is fairly simple to acquire it on-line on the IRS website. The office of Meissner, Joseph & Palley helps their clients go through the process.

SELLING PROBATE PROPERTY AND ASSETS

The personal representative has a fiduciary responsibility to marshal all assets or to acquire all assets the decedent owned. Some things are going to be really obvious. For example, if the decedent lived at 1234 Main Street, that's really easy to know if they  owned it or not. The personal representative is also going to look for bank accounts, stocks, bonds, or for any assets that would be an asset of the estate.

In a lot of cases, the person just doesn't know; maybe they weren't really that close to the decedent. In those cases, a couple of different things need to be done. Looking through bank statements is a good way to start and also looking at tax returns if they are available.

Another little know step the PR can take is they can have the accountant file with the IRS to get copies of the last few years' tax transcripts. That shows any entities that paid income to the decedent that has been reported to the IRS. That will include bank accounts that paid interest, stocks that paid dividends or many different assets. Anything reported to the IRS would show up in those tax transcripts so this can be a great tool to keep in mind.

The office of Meissner, Joseph & Palley has had cases where the tax transcripts have shown significant assets that the personal representative has then been able to marshal. In a unique case, the Personal Representative can even hire a private investigator to look even more in depth for assets. However, that's not common.

The Working Of A Probate Sale

The office of Meissner, Joseph & Palley has dealt with a lot of probate sales. Through the years they have worked with many real estate groups for probate sales of real estate.

In many ways, a probate sale of real estate is exactly like any other real estate sale in many ways. A listing agreement is signed just like when an individual sells the house. The main difference is that a probate listing agreement (California Association of Realtors Form PL) is used, not a standard listing agreement. When a buyer is found who wants to buy the house, they are asked to put their offer in on a probate sales agreement (California Association of Realtors Form PPA-CA). Instead of using the standard sales agreement, it's a probate sales agreement.

The California Association of Realtors has specific forms that are to be used for the sales agreement along with a few other mandatory forms. Once the person has put in their offer to buy the house and the administrator or executor has accepted the offer they now have a contract. An attorney's job is to then send out to all of the interested parties, all of the heirs, all of the beneficiaries, or anyone interested in this case, a "notice of proposed action" notifying them of this potential sale.

In the notice, the parties who received the Notice of Proposed Action are given a minimum of 15 days to object to the sale. If a person who has received that notice of proposed action feels that the sales price is too low, they can object. By  receiving an objection, the personal representative, with the help of the attorney, has to file documents in court and it becomes a court administered sale or probate court administered sale.

It is literally an auction and the auction is usually held about six weeks after it's been filed where the judge will formally announce the sale and bid. Occasionally, there is a bidding war in court and the price will move up. At the end of that process, after a court confirmation or if the notice of proposed action procedure is utilized, the personal representative signs all the closing documents and sells the house just like an individual. They then put the money into the probate estate account. If the total is more than $250,000 it is good practice to open bank accounts at different banks to ensure proper FDIC insurance.

The Sale Of Other Assets In Probate

The real estate probably has the most restrictions or rules on the seller of any assets that are sold during probate. There is a stricter appraisal process for real estate and the Notice requirements, discussed above, add protections. This is important as real estate is  subjective in value and often the most valuable asset in a probate estate. There is a wide range of what it could be worth, so having those protections in place is important. A lot of other things that sell during probate are either going to be of a very low value or have an obvious and set value determined by a market like a stock exchange. A person's household furniture, may have cost a lot, but is typically not worth very much. Nonetheless, care should be taken when selling the personal property also to both maximize the price and keep heirs informed.

Some items that are sold have a very clear and obvious value, for example, stocks that are publicly traded. Anybody can, if they want to sell their Ford Motor Company stock today, know exactly what it is worth. The process for selling those things is a lot simpler and typically, it is sold without any kind of notice to beneficiaries.

However, there could be situations where they are selling something that doesn't have an ascertainable value. Also, if the personal representative is concerned about the possibility of anyone contesting that sale or objecting to it, they can send out a notice of proposed action reciting the terms of the sale.

Attorneys will want to be extra cautious, and literally put everyone on notice of anything being sold if it has any kind of a subjective value to it. That would include cars, furniture, collectibles, or anything else of that nature.

THE FINAL PETITION IN THE PROBATE PROCESS

The first court date is about six weeks after filing and then that starts the four-month probate period. At the end of the four-month probate period, the final petition can be filed. If you are seeking that seven month probate, you are actually going to start working on the final  petition a couple of weeks before the four months end. Hopefully it can then be filed on the day those four months end and you get the court date about six weeks later.

However, you have to have completed everything required by the probate process before you file the file petition. In some cases, the real estate may have taken longer to sell, maybe research is still being done on heirs, maybe there are other assets the PR is looking for, whatever it might be. In those cases, it's best to wait until all of those things have been handled and then file the final petition.

Difference Between An Accounting
And Waiving An Accounting

A final petition in a probate court is going to tell the judge what has happened during the probate process, just like the initial petition tells the court who all the players are and what the money looks like. The final petition is going to lay out the facts to show what assets came in to the probate, what assets left the probate, what is left, and who it is to be distributed to.

In a lot of cases, the heirs or beneficiaries want to know how the money was spent. In those cases, a full accounting is going to be done. That accounting will show all the money that was received, exactly what was spent, what the attorney's fees are, what the administrator's fees are, what is left to distribute, and how it will be distributed.

However, if it's a case where everyone trusts each other you might be able to do a waiver of accounting. By waiving the accounting, the attorney and personal representative are able to get that final petition done more quickly and thus get it on file faster at the courthouse. The quicker they get that done, the quicker they are finishing probate, and the quicker they are writing checks.

It comes down to the heirs and beneficiaries, if they are comfortable with a summary of what's happened or if they want that full accounting to have every small detail on where the money went and why it is what it is.

The Approval Of The Final Petition

Once the final petition is approved, the judge signs the final order. The order says what should happen. The administrator's job or the executor's job is then to carry that out, write checks to the beneficiaries, the attorney, and to themselves. There also may be creditors who are paid in the final petition. Finally, they will  file all of the receipts at the courthouse and will get the final discharge. The final discharge is the document that officially ends the probate and closes the file at the courthouse.

THE ROLE OF AN ATTORNEY
IN THE PROBATE PROCESS

If the attorney is representing the personal representative, their role is to protect the PR and advise them of their fiduciary obligations. When an attorney starts a case, they are representing the personal representative as a fiduciary, not as an individual. The personal interest and the fiduciary interest  could be different for the client, but the attorney's job is to explain to them what the probate code says, what the case laws say, and what to expect in court.

The attorney's job is also to make sure that they are running for each hurdle and clearing the hurdles without any problems and looking ahead to try to avoid any problems that could be coming at them down the line. It's the attorney's job to accomplish each of those things.

If the attorney is representing a beneficiary, then their role is going to be a little different. They are going to be more like a watchdog, or the police, monitoring the probate to make sure the other attorney and the personal representative are doing their job right. If they are bumping into hurdles, the attorney will dig in and find out why, what may have been done wrong or figure out if they are doing something that is hurting the client, the beneficiary.

How Do Attorneys Minimize The Risk Of Delays?

An experienced attorney who has done many probates, will have an efficient system. They know what needs to be done to get a probate to the end in seven months. It starts with getting the initial documents done fast.  It means getting the client in, hopefully the same day from when they call, getting the documents prepared the same day and getting them filed in court the next day. It also means planning ahead.

The office of Meissner, Joseph & Palley has an elaborate calendaring system set up. The day letters are issued by the Court a number of calendar entries are triggered in the system. With that, they now have other targets that they're going to be looking out for to keep the process moving along. They are planning ahead, and they have it all calendared, to target that seven months period.

Attorneys also try to keep people informed to the extent they can. A lot of times, fights and problems come from people who are just not informed about what's going on. If an attorney informs them, it can sometimes avoid these issues.

Reasons A Beneficiary Or Heir
Might Want Their Own Attorney

Generally speaking, not everyone needs their own attorney. A lot of times, having multiple attorneys only causes problems.

People hire an attorney to represent them as a beneficiary, when they have concerns. The most common situation is a sibling working as the administrator or the executor and the beneficiary simply doesn't trust them. They may have specific reasons not to trust them or just general concerns. Hiring an attorney in those cases is good.

In some cases, the personal representative's attorney will not provide any information even after the beneficiary has asked or even after they filed a request for special notice. A lot of attorneys, right or wrong, will be more free with that information when talking to another attorney. Having an attorney represent you as a beneficiary might open up the dialogue a little bit.

Other situations, where an attorney could be helpful, would be where someone thinks they are an heir to an estate but they need to prove it. They don't want the estate to be distributed to someone else because they think they are entitled to something. Having an attorney represent you in those cases is important. Maybe there is

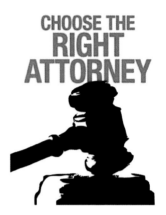

a newer will that should be probated. Maybe a will from 1999 has been filed for probate and you happen to know there is a will from 2016 that should be filed. This is a key time to hire an attorney!

Having an attorney to represent you can definitely help you and is important in a probate case for many reasons.

Some examples when a beneficiary or heir at law might want their own attorney:

1. Any time they have reason to believe, or are just concerned of the possibility, that the PR may steal from the estate;

2. If the PR's attorney will not provide any information even after you have filed a request for special notice;

3. You believe you are an heir at law and the PR and/or their attorney are not treating you as such;
4. You believe there is a different (newer) will that should be probated;
5. You believe the will being probated was signed under mistake, undue influence, or in some other fraudulent type situation;
6. You believe the will is a forgery and not actually signed by the decedent;
7. You want protections in place to make it harder for the PR to steal the estate;
8. You want an attorney on your side to explain everything to you from YOUR point of view;
9. You don't believe all assets have been included in the probate;
10. You just want to make sure things are done RIGHT.

When you visit the website for Meissner, Joseph & Palley at www.californiaprobate.info, they have a calculator where they list some of the common costs associated with probate. In the most common situation, when doing a full probate, they start with a $435 filing fee, which is standard for every case. After filing in Court they then have to publish in a newspaper.

Publication in the State of California ranges from about $50 in the cheapest county to $950 in some counties including several cities in Alameda County. This is the cost that you just can't get around. Then there is going to be a probate referee. That's  the person who is going to appraise all the assets. The probate referee is a state appointed official; they will appraise the assets. They are actually paid a percentage, around one-tenth of one percent. That cost can go up if it's a big case since it is based on the value of the assets.

There are always miscellaneous costs - a death certificate, certified copies at court and things like that. Lastly, there is a filing fee to end the probate, which is currently set at $435.

What If Someone Cannot Afford An Attorney?

If a person can't afford to hire an attorney, there is a form for requesting special notice. You can download that off the internet, send it to the attorney and the personal representative is supposed to keep you informed. You also can show up at court and advise the court of your concerns.

If you do not believe this person is equipped to be the personal representative then you may want to file an objection to them serving as PR. You can advise the judge and you can file written statements of your concerns in court. If you really do qualify as low income, there is a fee waiver form that you can fill out at the court where they will waive that $435 fee so you can file some written objections, which is really important to many people.

Trying To Navigate The Probate Process On Your Own

Anybody can do anything. The question really is how well will someone handle probate themselves and how many pitfalls will they accidentally fall into. Maybe they will cost themselves money and not even realize it. Certainly, it is possible to be your own attorney but the problem is that there are just too many little things to trip a person up and remember any glitch means it's another four-week, six-week, eight-week continuance. Then, before you know it the probate has been a year and a half.

Many times, people start the process on their own, and after wasting two long years, they contact the attorney and say, "You know, I tried to do it myself and that was a really huge mistake. I'd like to hire you now to finish the probate." In some of these cases, they are literally at ground zero. They still have seven months to go and in other cases, they are muddling along the process. So, it is possible to do the  probate yourself, but in most cases, a good probate attorney will be worth way more than their cost in value to you as the administrator or executor.